FONDUE

Simple and Delicious
FONDUE

Robert Carmack

APPLE

Contents

Introducing Fondue

Fondue has always been a communal affair. Diners revel in afixing small bits of bread or other morsels onto the tips of long forks and immersing them into the tabletop cauldrons. *Cuisine à la minute* never had a more precise meaning.

The word fondue is French for "melted." Traditional fondue is made of a blend of cheeses melted with alcohol but, today, vegetables, fruits, meat, and seafood fondues are also popular. Fondue can be divided into five categories: cheese, Burgundian, Bacchus, Asian and chocolate. For Burgundian fondue, raw meats and other foods are cooked at the table in rapidly simmering oil, then served with an array of dipping sauces. Bacchus fondue, named after the ancient god of wine, uses alcohol as the cooking medium. Asian fondues begin with either boiling water or broth, usually served in a distinct doughnut-shaped hot pot. Meat and vegetables are cooked at the table in the liquid, and the enriched broth is then served as a finale. This dish is variously known as a Mongolian hot pot, a firepot, or a steamboat. Chocolate fondue is a favorite for desserts.

Fondue, of course, is more than the liquid or sauce in the fondue pot. It is also the raw and blanched vegetables or cubed breads, meats, or fruits that are cooked or dipped in the fondue, as well as the dipping sauces served alongside. For example, a cheese fondue may be accompanied with pickled onions, boiled potatoes, and cucumbers, while Bacchus and Burgundian fondues are served with béarnaise sauce, mayonnaise, mustard, ketchup (tomato sauce), and chutney. Both fresh and dried fruits and cookies accompany chocolate fondues.

Four to six people is the optimum number at a fondue dinner. More than that results in too many people reaching too far across the table into too small a pot. Each diner should be equipped with a plate or bowl and, ideally, individual bowls of dipping sauce. While one fondue fork per person is adequate for a cheese fondue, meat fondues require a number of skewers, as guests will want to cook several pieces of meat at a time. Small wire-mesh skimmers, chopsticks, and tongs also come in handy for retrieving errant pieces of food.

RIGHT *Gingered dark chocolate fondue, see page 52*

Step-by-step Guide

Melting cheeses

The most common Swiss cheeses for fondue are Emmentaler and Gruyère. Although varying in flavor, other cheeses that melt particularly well are English Lancashire and Cheshire cheeses; Italian fontina, provolone, and mozzarella; and American jack cheese. Although a common addition to melting blends, and an essential ingredient in rarebit, Cheddar curdles easily and becomes grainy. Many blue-veined cheeses melt reasonably well.

The amount of food needed for your fondue will depend on whether you are serving one or more kinds of food. As a guide, below are suggested quantities per person:

CHEESE: 4–6 oz (125–185 g)
MEAT: 8 oz (250 g)
FISH AND SHELLFISH (shelled):
    6 oz (185 g)
BREAD: 1 loaf per 2–3 persons,
    or about twenty 1-inch (2.5-cm)
    cubes per person
VEGETABLES AND FRUIT: 6–8 oz
    (185–250 g) before trimming
FRUITS, DRIED AND FRESH: about
    2–4 oz (60–125 g) before peeling
    and coring
COOKIES (biscuits): about 4
CANDY (confection): about 4–6

1. Dice or coarsely shred the cheese.

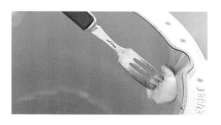

2. Rub the inside of a saucepan or fondue pot with a garlic clove. The garlic remnants may either be finely chopped and added to the pot, or discarded.

3. Heat the liquid, in this case wine and lemon juice, in a saucepan or as here, in a fondue pot. When the liquid is hot, reduce heat to low and add cheese.

4. Stir in a figure-8 movement to melt the cheese. Do not melt too quickly over too high a heat, or cheese will become tough and stringy.

 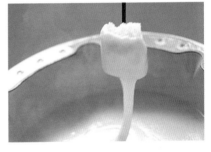

5. Dissolve potato flour or cornstarch (cornflour) in kirsch, vodka, or a similar distilled spirit. Stir into the fondue to bind and stabilize it, as well as to add flavor. Cook for a minute or two longer, adding ground pepper and freshly grated nutmeg.

6. If the fondue has been prepared in a saucepan, warm a fondue pot and pour mixture into it. Serve at the table, over a raised trivet and alcohol flame. (Note: a candle flame is insufficient.) Spear bread cubes onto long-handled fondue forks and dip into the cheese, swirling to coat neatly and to prevent dripping. Eat directly from the fork.

Heating oil, butter or ghee

While the traditional cheese fondue pot is made of stoneware, the high heat of simmering fat can crack this material. A cast iron or stainless steel pot is essential for cooking with oil, butter or ghee, the basis of Burgundian fondue. A few words of caution are needed for this style of cooking:

- Be vigilant when deep-frying at the table. When moist food comes in contact with hot oil, it literally explodes with vapor. For this reason, cook only a few pieces of food at a time. For tabletop deep-frying, use a slightly lower temperature than on a stove top. The oil should gently simmer, not boil.
- Never fill the pan more than one-third full of oil, butter, or ghee.
- Always stay close at hand when the fat is hot; never leave the pot unattended.
- Never shift or move a pot of hot fat.
- Remove skewers of food carefully from the oil to avoid dripping hot fat on the table or your partners.
- In case of a fire, do not douse with water. This can spread the flame. Instead, use a fire blanket or fire extinguisher.

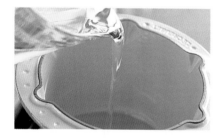

1. Fill a metal fondue pot no more than one-third full with oil, preferably grapeseed or peanut oil. At the table, heat oil to 325–350°F (165–175°C), or until simmering. Once the oil is hot, do not move the pot.

2. Spear a piece of vegetable or meat with a skewer, so that skewer protrudes by ½ inch (12 mm) at the other end. Skewer then rests on pan bottom, preventing food from touching the pot and sticking. Dip cooked food into sauces. Let oil cool completely before removing pot from the table.

Cooking with alcohol

Dry white acidic wines are most suited to cheese fondue, because the acid helps to prevent lumps. You may also add 1 teaspoon lemon juice per ⅓ cup wine to reinforce this tartness. Old-world wines, such as very dry Riesling or Italian Frascati, are also suitable, but floral New World wines rich in fruit, such as Chenin Blanc, oaky Chardonnay, and some Sauvignon Blancs, are less ideal. Similarly, a dry (hard) cider may be used, but most New World cider tends to be sweet and fruity. Red wine is not traditionally used in fondues.

Spirits used in Bacchus fondues are more variable, although generally dry by tradition. Sherry, Asian rice wines, even beer, ale, and stout may be used. The only restriction is alcohol content. Spirits may catch fire when heated, so they should not be used. Kirsch, a clear cherry distillate, is the most common liquor used in cheese fondue. Besides adding flavor, kirsch is also drunk during the meal, when it is called *le coup du milieu*, or "the mid-meal shot." Kirsch aficionados are wont to dip their bread into kirsh before the fondue pot.

Cook alcohol in pots made of stoneware or nonreactive metal. If using copper, make sure that it is well lined with tin, nickel, or stainless steel. Exposed patches of copper are toxic.

1. Pour just enough dry white wine into a fondue pot to fill by about two-thirds; heat to a rapid simmer. If desired, add 1 or 2 bouillon cubes for added flavor.

2. Thread vegetable or meat on a skewer, and plunge into simmering wine. Remove when cooked, drain, then dip into an assortment of accompanying sauces.

Cooking with charcoal

Traditionally, Asian fondues are cooked over charcoal. When burning any form of charcoal, always make sure that the room is well ventilated. Otherwise, carbon monoxide poisoning may occur. Always place the pot on a fireproof base such as bricks or a stone slab. If there is a likelihood that the heat will conduct through the bricks onto the table, place a fireproof mat under the base.

1. Light a small pile of lump or natural charcoal in a fireplace or in an outdoor grill. Natural charcoal is preferable to charcoal briquettes because it's pure and burns at a higher temperature. Mound the charcoal around an electric fire starter, plug it in, and after 7 minutes remove the starter. Alternatively, light charcoal in a charcoal chimney: tightly wad newspaper in its base, place charcoal on top, and set the newspaper alight. Do not use instant lighter liquids, firesticks, and other chemical fire agents, as these may produce unpleasant fumes at the table. Never use gasoline or kerosene, as both are dangerously explosive. Pour hot broth into a firepot or metal fondue pot to fill it by about two-thirds.

2. Once the coals are covered with a layer of white ash, after about 20 minutes, use long-handled metal tongs to transfer them into the chimney of the pot. Wear a heavy oven mitt in case some charcoal falls and requires quick retrieval. Add hot coals to the center of the chimney pot, filling it no more than halfway. Bring the broth to a rapid simmer.
NOTE If the pot has a lid attached to the chimney stack, remove it during cooking; cover to douse the flame. Conversely, many models have a ring lid for the stock; this should be in place to sufficiently raise the broth temperature prior to cooking.

3. Use small wire-mesh skimmers, chopsticks, and tongs to dip raw foods into and retrieve cooked foods from the broth, and dip them into the sauces. After guests have finished eating the meat and vegetables, add cooked rice or soaked noodles to the broth. Heat through and ladle into soup bowls. However, some broths, such as Vietnamese lau, are too pungent to eat as soup.

Melting chocolate

Always use a good grade of chocolate, preferably couverture, and melt it over low heat, to prevent burning. Steam and droplets of water must be avoided when melting chocolate, or it will seize into a stiff mass. Melt milk chocolate at a lower temperature than pure chocolate. To melt chocolate in a microwave, cook chocolate, uncovered, at 70 per cent for 1 minute at a time, or until it looks half melted; stir until smooth.

1. Chop chocolate into small pieces. Place liquid ingredients of recipe in a double boiler or in a heatproof bowl in a saucepan, over barely simmering water. Add all the chocolate and stir until it is melted and combined. (Do not melt chocolate before adding to liquid, as it may seize, or over a direct flame, because chocolate burns easily.)

2. Set a fondue pot over a candle flame or Bunsen burner to warm, but do not overheat or the chocolate will burn when added. Alternatively, rinse a fondue pot in hot water, dry carefully and keep in a warm spot until needed. Then pour chocolate into the warmed fondue pot.

Cheese Fondues

With cheese fondue, cubes of bread and sometimes pieces of boiled potato, vegetables, and cooked meats are dipped in a luscious cheese sauce. Ideally, a classic cheese fondue requires well-aged imported Swiss cheese such as Emmentaler or Gruyère. Most New World Swiss-style cheeses, however, are seldom sufficiently matured to make a classic fondue. Just as Cheddar is commonly available as mild, sharp, and extra sharp in English-speaking countries, Gruyère and Emmentaler come in varying degrees of pungency when sold in the Alps. The subtle blending of these different cheese flavors is a distinguishing characteristic of Swiss fondues.

In England, America, and other English-speaking countries, a wide assortment of cheeses can be used in melted-cheese dishes. Olde England and colonial America both produced versions of rarebit, or rabbit, sometimes substituting strong ale or stout for Continental wines. Feta and other fresh sheep's- and goat's-milk cheeses, including blue-veined varieties, melt

sufficiently when bound with either flour or cornstarch (cornflour). To make the nacho-like fondue spiked with chopped green chilies, Monterey Jack may be used as a substitute for the Mexican cheeses of asadero or queso Chihuahua. Mozzarella is also a suitable substitute.

RIGHT Welsh rarebit, see page 22

14

Classic Neuchâtel fondue

Serves 4–6

1 clove garlic

1 cup (8 fl oz/250 ml) dry white wine

10 oz (300 g) Emmentaler cheese, diced or shredded

10 oz (300 g) Gruyère cheese, diced or shredded

1 1/2 tablespoons potato flour or cornstarch (cornflour)

mixed with 1/4 cup (2 fl oz/60 ml) kirsch

1/4 teaspoon ground white pepper

pinch of freshly grated nutmeg

crusty bread, cut into cubes, for serving

Rub a medium, heavy saucepan with garlic. Either discard garlic pieces or finely chop them and add to the saucepan. Place pot over medium-high heat, add wine and bring just to a boil. Immediately reduce heat to low and add cheese, stirring slowly in a figure-8 pattern until cheese is just melted. It should melt very slowly—about 5 minutes in all—otherwise, it may become stringy and tough. Add potato flour or cornstarch mixture, pepper, and nutmeg to the cheese mixture. Simmer for about 2 minutes more. The fondue should gently sputter, not boil. (The fondue should be thick enough to just cover the bread; it will thicken at the table.)

Pour the fondue into a warmed fondue pot and serve immediately. At the table, guests should take several cubes of bread onto their plates, skewer one with a fork, and dip it into the pot, twirling gently to prevent drips. Eat directly from the fork.

Green fondue with fresh herbs

Serves 4–6
1 small clove garlic
1 cup (8 fl oz/250 ml) medium-dry white wine
1 tablespoon fresh lemon juice
1 1/4 lb (625 g) Edam or Gouda cheese, shredded
1 tablespoon potato flour or cornstarch (cornflour)
1/4 cup (1/4 oz/7 g) chopped fresh parsley
2 tablespoons chopped fresh chives
2 teaspoons dried tarragon
pinch of cayenne pepper
1/2 teaspoon ground white pepper
1 tablespoon gin
slices of crusty bread, raw vegetables, and cooked meats of choice, for serving

Rub a medium, heavy saucepan with garlic clove. Add wine and bring just to a boil. Add lemon juice, and immediately lower heat to medium-low. Toss cheese with the potato flour or cornstarch, then add it to the pot handful by the handful, stirring with each addition until just melted. Add herbs, seasonings, and gin. Cook for 2–3 minutes, then transfer to a warmed fondue pot. Serve with the bread, vegetables, and meats alongside.

Crab and Cheddar fondue

Serves 4–6
3/4 cup (6 fl oz/180 ml) hard (dry) cider or beer
1 tablespoon fresh lemon juice
pinch of sugar
1 lb (500 g) sharp (tasty) Cheddar cheese, shredded
2 tablespoons all-purpose (plain) flour
7 oz (220 g) fresh lump crabmeat, picked over for shell
1 teaspoon caraway seed, lightly toasted
1/2 teaspoon salt, or to taste
pinch of cayenne pepper
cubes of crusty bread, for serving

In a double boiler over simmering water, heat the cider or beer, lemon juice, and sugar. Meanwhile, toss cheese with the flour. When liquid is hot, reduce heat, gradually stir in cheese, and let it melt slowly, about 5 minutes. Meanwhile, heat

crabmeat in a microwave on medium high until warm, about 30 seconds. (This helps prevent the cheese from curdling later.) Add crabmeat, caraway seed, salt, and cayenne to the melted cheese. Transfer to a warm fondue pot and serve with the bread cubes alongside.

Fondue Mexicana

Serves 4–6
1 cup (8 fl oz/250 ml) beer
1 tablespoon fresh lemon juice
6 small fresh chilies, seeded and coarsely chopped
1/2 bell pepper (capsicum), seeded and diced
1 lb (500 g) Monterey Jack or mild mozzarella cheese, shredded
2 tablespoons all-purpose (plain) flour
1/2 teaspoon paprika
pinch of ground cumin
1 teaspoon salt, or to taste
tortilla chips, for serving

In a heavy, medium saucepan, heat beer over high heat until it foams. Add lemon juice, chilies and bell pepper. Reduce heat to medium. Toss cheese with the flour, paprika, and cumin, then add to the pan, 1 handful at a time, stirring to melt each handful. Add salt. Transfer to a warm fondue pot. Serve with the tortilla chips alongside.

NOTE Wash your hands, knife and chopping board well with hot, soapy water after touching the chilies, as their lingering oils will burn the skin. Avoid touching your skin, eyes, and nose when handling chili. Fresh chilies contain volatile oils that can burn skin and tender membranes.

Welsh rarebit

Serves 4–6
¹/₂ cup (4 oz/125 g) butter
¹/₂ cup (4 fl oz/125 ml) beer or ale
1 lb (500 g) extra sharp (extra tasty) Cheddar or Lancashire cheese, shredded
salt to taste
¹/₂ teaspoon ground white pepper
1–2 loaves toasted bread slices, each cut into 4 triangles, for serving

In a medium saucepan, combine butter and beer or ale. Heat over medium heat until bubbles appear. Reduce heat to medium-low and add the cheese all at once, stirring until just melted. Add salt and pepper. Pour into a warmed fondue pot. Serve with toast. Use either forks or fingers to dip the bread.

Stout rabbit

Serves 4–6
³/₄ cup (6 oz/180 g) butter
²/₃ cup (5 fl oz/150 ml) stout or porter
1 tablespoon all-purpose (plain) flour
1 lb (500 g) Stilton or blue cheese, crumbled
1 tablespoon prepared English (hot) mustard
¹/₂ teaspoon ground white pepper
1–2 loaves thin French bread, thinly sliced and toasted, for serving

In a medium saucepan, combine butter and stout or porter. Heat over low heat to melt the butter. Whisk in flour, then gradually add the cheese a little at a time, stirring just until melted. Add mustard and pepper. Pour into a warmed fondue pot. Serve with toast squares, using either fingers or a fork to dip the bread.

RIGHT *Stout rabbit*

Blue cheese fondue

Serves 4–6
1/2 cup (4 oz/125 g) unsalted butter
2 shallots (French shallots), very finely chopped
1 clove garlic, finely chopped
1 cup (8 fl oz/250 ml) dry white wine
1 lb (500 g) blue cheese, crumbled
3 egg yolks
1/2 cup (4 fl oz/125 ml) Enriched meat stock, heated (see page 56)
1/2 teaspoon dried tarragon
1 tablespoon Dijon mustard
1/4 teaspoon salt
1/4 teaspoon ground pepper
rye bread and/or sourdough bread cubes, gherkins or cornichons,
and pickled onions, for serving

In a medium, heavy saucepan, melt butter over medium-low heat. Sauté shallots and garlic until translucent, about 3 minutes. Add white wine, increase heat to medium and cook to reduce to a glaze, about 20 minutes. Sit the pan over a pot of simmering water. Stir in cheese until melted. Whisk egg yolks with the hot stock, then stir briskly into the melted cheese; add remaining ingredients. Continue cooking until slightly thickened; do not overcook or boil, or it may curdle. Immediately strain into a warm fondue pot and place over very low heat to keep warm. Serve with bread and pickles.

Burgundian Fondues

Burgundian fondue is actually Swiss in origin. Although there appears to be no clear historical link between Burgundy and oil-bathed food cooked at the table, one anecdote is that a Swiss restaurateur had a restaurant in that part of France, and later, when he relocated to Switzerland, he coined the term "fondue bourguignonne." The closest similarity is when Mexicans refer to a dish as "Swiss" simply because it is cooked with cream, and when the English or the French call a style "Indian" because it is flavored with curry powder.

With Burgundian fondue, a metal pot (either stainless steel or cast iron) is best suited. Pieces of raw meat are cooked in simmering fat, then dipped in an assortment of dipping sauces. Since the meat cooks in a matter of minutes, it should be cubed from tender cuts: beef tenderloin; boneless, skinless chicken breast; pork and lamb tenderloin. The exception is flank steak (skirt steak), which is cut into thin slices. To use slow-cooking vegetables, parboil them in advance. Skewers are preferred to forks for Burgundian fondues, as they allow diners to pierce through the meat, letting the skewer protrude ½ inch (12 mm) at the other end. The skewer can then rest on the bottom of the pot, which keeps the meat from sticking to the pot.

Either oil, clarified butter or ghee may be used as the cooking medium for a Burgundian fondue. Use a good-quality oil such as grapeseed or peanut, as these withstand high temperatures without smoking. Clarified butter also withstands frying temperatures without burning (see recipe page 56). Ghee is an easy substitute, available in cans from any Asian or Indian grocer, and in the gourmet aisles of many supermarkets. Take special care when cooking with oil, melted butter or ghee at the table, as nasty burns occur from a single drop.

A typical Burgundian fondue comes with béarnaise sauce, mayonnaise and condiments such as mustard, ketchup (tomato sauce), and chutney. After cooking, the pieces of food are dipped into a spicy sauce, followed by a hot dip, followed by another sour, one sweet, and so on.

RIGHT *Fundamentally bourguignonne, see page 28*

Fundamentally bourguignonne

Serves 6

3 lb (1.5 kg) veal loin or beef tenderloin (fillet), trimmed
parsley sprigs, for garnish
3–5 cups (24–40fl oz/750 ml–1.25 L) grapeseed or peanut oil, or Clarified butter
(see page 56) or ghee, melted, or a combination
salt and freshly ground pepper to taste
Mounted béarnaise (see page 55) plus other dipping sauces of choice, for serving
salad, pickled onions, olives and bread, for serving

Cut meat into ¾-inch (2-cm) cubes and arrange on a platter. Garnish with parsley, cover and refrigerate. Meanwhile, fill a fondue pot no more than one-third with the oil, butter and/or ghee. At the table, heat to 325–350°F (165–175°C). Sprinkle the meat with salt and pepper. Secure a piece of meat onto a skewer, with the skewer protruding by ½ inch (12 mm), and cook until the desired doneness, 2–3 minutes.

Remove meat from the oil. Serve with the dipping sauces alongside. Accompany with a mushroom or green salad, pickled onions, olives, and bread. Wait until the oil, butter, or ghee has cooled completely before removing the pot from the table.

Beef with spice rub

Serves 6

1 tablespoon juniper berries

1 tablespoon peppercorns

1 teaspoon whole allspice

1/4 teaspoon ground (powdered) ginger

1/2 teaspoon dry (powdered) mustard

2 bay leaves, crumbled

1/4 cup (2 oz/60 g) coarse salt

3 lb (1.5 kg) beef flank (skirt) steak, trimmed

parsley sprigs, for garnish

3–5 cups (24–40 fl oz/750 ml–1.25 L) grapeseed or peanut oil

Mounted béarnaise (see page 54) or other dipping sauces of choice, for serving

In a mortar, combine juniper berries, peppercorns, allspice, ginger and mustard. Grind to a coarse powder. Stir in bay leaves and salt. Pat all over the beef. Cover and refrigerate for 2–3 hours. When ready to serve, scrape off seasoning and thinly slice meat across the grain. Arrange slices on a serving platter and garnish with parsley. Pour oil into a metal fondue pot, filling it no more than one-third full. At the table, heat oil to 325–350°F (165–175°C). Thread meat on skewers, letting them protrude by 1/2 inch (12 mm). Cook until the desired doneness, about 1 minute. Remove from the pot and dip into sauces. Let oil cool before removing the pot from the table.

Garlic shrimp

Serves 4–6

36 raw jumbo shrimp (king prawns),
    about 2 lb (1 kg), shelled and
    deveined (tails left on)
1 whole bulb garlic
1 teaspoon red chili pepper flakes
1/3 cup (3 fl oz/90 ml) olive oil

1/4 cup (2 fl oz/60 ml) dry white wine
1 teaspoon salt
3–5 cups (11/2–21/2 lb/750 g–1.25 kg)
    Clarified butter (see page 56)
Quick ponzu (see page 56) plus other
    dipping sauces of choice
slices of crusty or toasted bread

Score the underside of each shrimp with 2 or 3 shallow slashes to prevent curling. Separate cloves from the garlic bulb and peel half of them; finely chop. Reserve unpeeled cloves to flavor the oil. Combine chopped garlic, pepper flakes, oil, wine, and salt. Add shrimp and toss to coat. Cover and refrigerate for 2–3 hours. When ready to serve, drain the shrimp. Arrange them on a platter and bring to the table.

Fill a metal fondue pot one-third full with clarified butter. Add unpeeled garlic. At the table, heat to 325–350°F (165–175°C). Skewer a shrimp through

each end, letting skewer protrude by 1/2 inch (12 mm). Plunge shrimp into hot oil and cook until pink, about 2 minutes. Remove and drain. Serve with dipping sauces. When garlic cloves soften and become lightly golden, about 20 minutes, remove from the oil and press onto bread slices. Let butter or ghee cool completely before removing the pot from the table.

Curried fish strips

Serves 6

2 lb (1 kg) firm white fish fillets, such as cod, flounder or halibut

1 cup (5 oz/150 g) all-purpose (plain) flour

1/2 teaspoon cayenne pepper

2 tablespoons curry powder

1 teaspoon salt

3–6 eggs

3–5 cups (24–40 fl oz/750 ml–1.25 L) grapeseed or peanut oil, or Clarified butter (see page 56) or ghee, melted or a combination

Mounted béarnaise (see page 55), Curried mayonnaise (see page 57), bottled tartare sauce and/or soy sauce, for dipping

Cut fish into strips 2 inches (5 cm) long, 1 inch (2.5 cm) wide, and 1/2 inch (12 mm) thick. Thread onto skewers, letting skewer protrude by 1/2 inch (12 mm).

Sift flour, cayenne, curry powder, and salt together. Dredge fish in flour mixture and place on a tray, with waxed paper between layers, and refrigerate until ready to serve, up to 6 hours.

Place 1 egg in each serving bowl and lightly beat. Fill a metal fondue pot one-third full with oil, butter, or ghee. At the table, heat to 325–350°F (165–175°C).

Dip skewers with fish in the egg, drain, and plunge into the hot oil. (If bowls are too shallow, use a pastry brush to coat fish.) Fry until lightly golden, about 2 minutes. If fish pieces overcook and break during cooking, use a small wire-mesh skimmer or slotted spoon to retrieve them. Dip cooked fish into desired dipping sauce.

Vinegar-dipped potatoes

Serves 6

2 lb (1 kg) unpeeled small new potatoes (chats), well scrubbed
1 1/2 cups (12 fl oz/375 ml) apple cider vinegar
1 cup (8 fl oz/250 ml) peanut or
olive oil
1/2 cup (4 oz/125 g) butter
1 large onion, finely chopped
2 teaspoons whole caraway or cumin seed
2 teaspoons salt
1/2 teaspoon ground pepper
mustard, horseradish, Anchovy sauce (see page 54), Curried mayonnaise
(see page 57), or sauces of choice

Cook potatoes in salted boiling water until barely tender, 8–10 minutes. Drain. Meanwhile, combine all ingredients, except sauce, in a saucepan. Bring to a boil, reduce heat, and simmer 5 minutes. Transfer to a warmed nonreactive fondue pot and add potatoes. At the table, simmer potatoes until tender but not overcooked, about 20 minutes. Prick potato to determine doneness. (Unlike other Burgundian fondues, the potatoes are not fried; the large quantity of vinegar flavoring the oil prevents that.) Skewer potatoes with fondue forks, and dip into individual bowls of sauce.

Greek lamb fondue

Serves 6

3 lb (1.5 kg) lamb loin or boneless leg, cut into ¾-inch (2-cm) cubes
¼ cup (2 fl oz/60 ml) lemon juice
⅓ cup (3 fl oz/90 ml) olive oil
2 teaspoons dried oregano
1 teaspoon dried finely chopped garlic
1 teaspoon salt
fresh oregano, for garnish and for frying (optional)
3–5 cups (24–40 fl oz/750 ml–1.25 L) grapeseed or peanut oil
or Clarified butter (see page 56) or ghee; melted or a combination
4 unpeeled cloves garlic
slices of crusty (or toasted) bread, mint jelly, Mounted béarnaise (see page 55),
Anchovy sauce (see page 54) and other sauces, for serving

Toss lamb with lemon juice, olive oil, oregano, and garlic. Cover and refrigerate for 2–3 hours. Toss in salt. Garnish with fresh oregano, if using. Fill a metal fondue pot one-third full with oil, clarified butter, ghee, or a combination. At the table, heat to 325–350°F (165–175°C). Add garlic cloves and oregano, if using, but remove when browned. Discard oregano and spread garlic on the bread. Insert skewers into lamb cubes, letting the skewer protrude by ½ inch (12 mm). Plunge lamb into the pot. Cook until the desired doneness, 2–3 minutes. Serve with dipping sauces.

Bacchus Fondues

Bacchus fondues use wine in place of oil. The same cuts of meat are used as for Burgundian fondues, but the meats are usually cut into thin strips and threaded onto skewers. Either a stoneware or a metal pot may be used. White wine is the classic cooking medium, which can be flavored with a bouillon cube or fresh herbs. Sherry, beer, and rice wine may also be used for cooking, but high-proof spirits may not, as they become flammable when heated. Either fondue forks or skewers may be used to spear or thread the pieces of food. As with Burgundian fondue, after cooking the food is dipped into one or more sauces.

La Gitana

Serves 4–6

2 lb (1 kg) boneless, skinless chicken breasts

1 lb (500 g) veal or pork tenderloin

1 teaspoon salt (optional)

vegetable crudités of choice

4–5 cups (32–40 fl oz/1–1.25 L) dry sherry

1–2 beef bouillon (stock) cubes (optional)

Mounted béarnaise sauce (see page 55) and Anchovy sauce (see page 54), or dipping sauces of choice

Slice chicken into thin strips. Cut veal into ¾-inch (2-cm) pieces; cut pork slightly smaller. Arrange meats on separate platters and lightly salt the pork, if using; cover and refrigerate. Arrange vegetables on a separate platter, cover, and refrigerate until ready to use. Fill a stoneware or metal fondue pot about two-thirds full with the sherry and add bouillon cube(s), if using. At the table, heat to a rapid simmer. (Or measure the required amount, heat on the stove, and transfer to the fondue pot.) Secure meat onto wooden skewers, letting the end of the skewer protrude by ½ inch (12 mm). Plunge meat into the pot and cook for 3–7 minutes (chicken, veal and pork should not be rare). Repeat with vegetables, cooking until desired doneness. Serve with individual bowls of sauce.

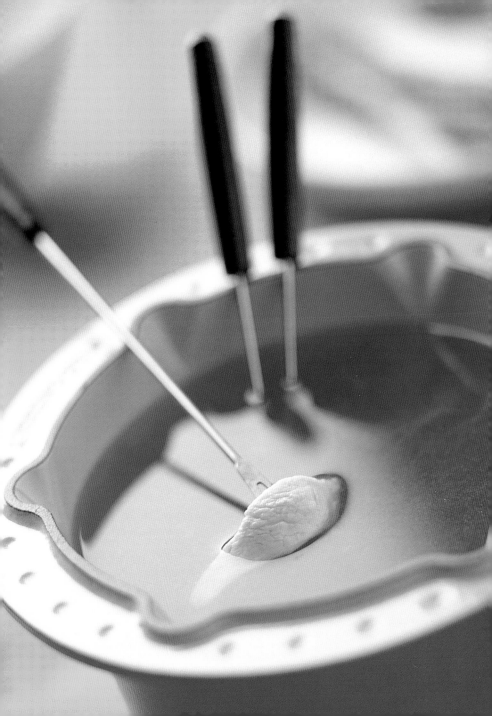

A fondue of marinated meats

Serves 4–6
3 lb (1.5 kg) beef rib eye steak (Scotch fillet), trimmed
3 tablespoons white wine vinegar
¼ cup (2 fl oz/60 ml) olive or good-quality salad or vegetable oil
¼ cup (2 fl oz/60 ml) dry white wine
1 clove garlic, crushed
1 shallot (French shallot), finely chopped
1 teaspoon salt
2 teaspoons coarsely ground pepper
vegetable crudités of choice
4–5 cups (32–40 fl oz/1–1.25 L) dry white wine
Mounted béarnaise sauce (see page 55) or other dipping sauces of choice
crusty bread and green salad

Cut beef into thin strips. Combine white wine vinegar, olive, salad or vegetable
oil, white wine, garlic, shallot, salt and pepper in a shallow dish and toss with
the beef. Cover and refrigerate for at least 2 hours or overnight.

Place vegetables on a platter; cover and refrigerate until ready to bring to the
table. Fill a stoneware or metal fondue pot two-thirds full with the wine. At the
table, bring just to a rapid simmer. (Alternatively, measure the required amount,
heat on the stove, and transfer to the fondue pot.) Drain beef and place it in a
shallow serving dish. Thread meat on skewers and spear the vegetables, letting
the end of each skewer protrude by ½ inch (12 mm). Cook the meat 2–3
minutes, and the vegetables 3–5 minutes. Remove from the wine and dip into
individual bowls of sauce. Accompany with crusty bread and green salad.

Seafood in court bouillon

Serves 6

1 lb (500 g) raw medium shrimp
(prawns), shelled (tails left on and
shells reserved)

10-oz (300-g) jar fresh oysters

1 can (14 oz/440 g) abalone (optional)

12 oz (375 g) scallops or squid
(calamari) rings

36 small clams, scrubbed

1 1/2 lb (750 g) firm white fish fillets
such as cod, perch, or halibut, cut
into bite-sized pieces

Quick ponzu (see page 57), for dipping

FOR COURT BOUILLON

5 cups (40 fl oz/1.25 L) water

reserved ingredients from left

2 carrots, peeled and coarsely chopped

1 onion, diced

4 sprigs parsley

1 teaspoon dried thyme

2 bay leaves

1/2 teaspoon peppercorns

1 teaspoon salt

1 clove garlic, crushed

pinch of cayenne pepper

1 1/2 cups (12 fl oz/375 ml) white wine

crusty bread, for serving

Combine all court bouillon ingredients in a large nonreactive saucepan, cover and bring to a boil. Remove lid, reduce heat and simmer for 20 minutes. When ready to serve, strain and transfer to a fondue pot, maintaining a gentle simmer, about 325–350°F (160–175°C). The liquid should fill two-thirds of the pot. If not, add boiling water.

Remove shrimp vein and gently score the underside of shrimp to prevent curling. Drain oysters. (Reserve liquor for the bouillon.) Drain the abalone, if using, (add its juice to the bouillon), and slice paper-thin. Arrange seafood on a platter, cover, and refrigerate until required.

Dip seafood into simmering broth. Cook shrimp about 3 minutes. The clams are done when open, 2–3 minutes; discard any that do not open. Cook white fish until white throughout, about 2 minutes. Cook scallops until just opaque, 1–2 minutes. The squid will take about 1 minute, and the oysters 30 seconds. Add the abalone at the end and cook about 30 seconds to just heat through. Do not overcook seafood, or it will be tough. Remove from broth and dip into sauce. Serve with cups of the cooking liquid, crusty bread, finger bowls and towels.

Asian Fondues

Asian fondues have a plethora of names: hoh go, shabu shabu, lau, and sin sul lo. In the West, they are variously called Mongolian hot pots, firepots and steamboats. Asian fondues are traditionally cooked in a large, doughnut-shaped pot. The larger circumference of the pot allows for the simultaneous cooking of more foods than a smaller pot. The broth becomes richer with the addition of each meat and vegetable, and after all the pieces of food have been cooked and eaten, cooked rice or noodles are added to the concentrated broth, then ladled out into small bowls as a delicious finale.

Shabu shabu

Serves 6

3 lb (1.5 kg) well-marbled beef
  tenderloin (fillet) or sirloin
1 lb (500 g) soft tofu, cut into 3/4–1 inch
  (2–2.5 cm) cubes, rinsed
1 bunch scallions (shallots/spring onions),
  bias-cut into 2-inch (5-cm) pieces

1/4 head Chinese napa cabbage
2 carrots, peeled and cut into thin rounds
1 bunch spinach or chrysanthemum
  leaves, stemmed
8-inch (20-cm) piece konbu
Quick ponzu (see page 57), for dipping
steamed rice, for serving

Cut meat wafer-thin across the grain. Arrange slices on a platter or individual plates. Cover and refrigerate until needed. Soak tofu in water for 20 minutes; drain. Arrange tofu and vegetables on a platter. Wipe konbu with a damp cloth to remove any grit. Place konbu in a Japanese donabe or fondue pot (if using a coal firepot, see page 12 for instructions). Fill two-thirds full with cold water. (It is essential to add the liquid before heating the pot; otherwise, the solder joins of the pot might melt from the heat of the coals.) At the table, bring to a simmer and remove konbu. Swish pieces of meat in the simmering broth to the desired doneness, about 10 seconds. Dip into ponzu. Place vegetable pieces in the broth until done, 2–5 minutes. Remove. Serve with bowls of steamed rice.

Chicken mizutaki

Serves 6

3 lb (1.5 kg) boneless, skinless chicken thighs
and breasts, cut into bite-sized pieces
20 dried black (shiitake) mushrooms
1/2 bunch scallions (shallots/spring onions)
1 bunch asparagus, trimmed
1 green bell pepper (capsicum), seeded
1/4 head Chinese napa cabbage
2 carrots, peeled and cut into thin rounds
1/4 cauliflower, broken into small florets, stems peeled and sliced
1 head broccoli, broken into small florets, stems peeled and sliced
4–6 cups (32–48 fl oz/1–1.5 L) Chicken broth (see page 54)
Mizutaki sauce (see page 56) or Quick ponzu (see page 57), for dipping
steamed rice, for serving

Put chicken pieces in a sieve. Pour boiling water over them and drain. Let cool. Arrange pieces on a serving platter. Cover and refrigerate until ready to serve.

Soak mushrooms in warm water for 20 minutes, or until soft. Drain. Use scissors to snip off the tough stems; discard. Cut scallions and asparagus into 2-inch (5-cm) lengths. Cut the bell pepper into 2-inch-long sticks. Arrange vegetables in groups attractively on a platter and cover; refrigerate until ready to serve.

To serve, pour broth into a Japanese donabe or a fondue pot, filling it about two-thirds full. (If using a coal firepot, refer to page 12 for instructions.) At the table, bring to a rapid simmer. Add vegetables as desired, retrieving loose vegetable pieces with a small wire-mesh skimmer. Use chopsticks to dip pieces of chicken in the broth and cook until done, no less than 3 minutes. Accompany with dipping sauces and eat with bowls of steamed rice. When finished, ladle the broth into the rice bowls.

Vietnamese lau

Serves 6

2 packets (40 sheets) round rice paper

1 medium onion, thinly sliced

1 tablespoon rice vinegar or distilled white vinegar

3 lb (1.5 kg) eye of beef round, sirloin, or tenderloin (fillet), trimmed and cut into paper-thin slices

2 tablespoons Asian sesame oil

2 teaspoons coarsely ground pepper

3 heads butter (Boston) lettuce, leaves washed and separated

1 telegraph or long cucumber, peeled, halved lengthwise and seeded

1 bunch scallions (shallots/spring onions), cut into 2-inch (5-cm) lengths

4 oz (125 g) bean sprouts

sprigs from 1 bunch fresh mint

1 bunch fresh cilantro (fresh coriander)

1 bunch Thai or sweet basil

2 tablespoons peanut oil

2 garlic cloves, thinly sliced

1-inch (2.5-cm) piece fresh ginger, thinly sliced

1 stalk lemongrass, white part only, cut into thin rounds (optional)

1 cup (8 fl oz/250 ml) rice vinegar or distilled white vinegar

5 cups (40 fl oz/1.25 L) water

1 tablespoon salt

3 tablespoons sugar

1 cup (5 oz/150 g) peanuts (ground nuts), crushed, for serving

Nuoc cham sauce (see page 55), for dipping

Cover rice paper with a damp cloth and wrap with plastic wrap until needed. About 1 hour before the meal, dip each rice paper in warm water for 10 seconds to soften. Stack, interspersing each rice paper with well-moistened waxed paper, and wrap stack in plastic wrap to prevent drying. Should they stick together, brush liberally with water at the table.

In a small bowl, toss onion with vinegar. Arrange beef on 2 platters, overlapping as little as possible. Drizzle with oil and sprinkle with pepper. Drain onions, discarding vinegar, and break onion slices into rings. Place decoratively over meat. Cover and refrigerate until ready to serve.

Tear any large lettuce leaves in half and cut away any stiff cores (they can tear rice paper when rolled). Cut cucumber into very thin semi-circles. Arrange all vegetables on a serving platter. Cover and refrigerate until ready to serve.

In a large saucepan, heat oil over medium heat. Add garlic and ginger and sauté until fragrant, 1–2 minutes. Do not let garlic brown. Add lemongrass, vinegar, water, salt, and sugar. Bring to a rapid simmer. Strain broth into hot pot or metal fondue pot on the table. Broth should fill the pot about two-thirds full; if not, add boiling water. Bring to a rapid simmer.

To serve, lay a sheet of rice paper on a plate and top with a lettuce leaf, a few herb sprigs, and some onions. Drop a piece of meat into the simmering liquid until the desired doneness, about 10 seconds. Retrieve with chopsticks or a wire-mesh skimmer. Lay meat over vegetables. If desired, sprinkle with ground peanuts, then fold to enclose the bottom and top. Roll up. (If papers tear, fold sheets in half to a double thickness, and roll, leaving the two ends exposed.) The finished roll should be the size of a thick cigar. Dip in Nuoc cham sauce and eat with your fingers.

Mongolian firepot

Serves 6

12 oz (375 g) flank steak (skirt steak)
12 oz (375 g) boneless lean lamb
2 tablespoons soy sauce
2 tablespoons Asian sesame oil
1/2-inch (12-mm) piece fresh ginger, grated
1 small clove garlic, crushed
4 boneless, skinless chicken breast halves, thinly sliced
1 lb (500 g) soft tofu, cut into 3/4-inch (2-cm) cubes
4 oz (125 g) mushrooms
2 turnips or 1 rutabaga (Swede), peeled
1/2 bunch spinach, stemmed
leaves from 1/4 head Chinese napa cabbage
4 oz (125 g) snow peas (mange-tout), trimmed
1 bunch scallions (shallots/spring onions), cut into 2-inch (5-cm) pieces
4–6 cups (32–48 fl oz/1–1.5 L) Enriched meat stock (page 56)
2 tablespoons rice wine or dry sherry
Mongolian firepot dip (see page 57)
condiments of choice, such as plum, hoisin, and satay sauce
4 oz (125 g) cellophane (bean thread) noodles

Cut beef and lamb into paper-thin slices and lay them slightly overlapping on platters or individual plates. In a medium bowl, combine soy sauce, sesame oil, ginger, and garlic. Add chicken and toss to coat. Arrange chicken on a separate platter. Wrap and refrigerate meat and chicken until ready to use.

Soak tofu in water for 20 minutes, then drain. Halve any large mushrooms. Cut turnips or rutabaga into thin strips about 2 inches (5 cm) long. Arrange vegetables decoratively on a serving platter or plates. Prepare coals for a firepot, if using (see page 12 for instructions). Add stock and wine to a firepot or a metal fondue pot. Bring to a rapid simmer. At the table, have guests individually cook their meats and vegetables. Meats will cook in 10–20 seconds. Spinach will cook within 10 seconds, but other vegetables may take 2 minutes or longer. Serve with steamed rice, moistened with a little cooking broth. Midway through the meal, soak noodles in hot water for 10 minutes; drain and set aside. When guests have finished the meat and vegetables, add the noodles to the cooking broth. Ladle bowls of broth and noodles for each diner.

Chocolate Fondues

Chocolate fondues arrived late on the scene, originating in the 1950s as a dish using Toblerone, a well-known Swiss brand. Reportedly the creation of a New York publicist for that chocolate company, the dish was then embraced by a Swiss restaurant in New York frequented by embassy staff and expatriates alike. When they, in turn, headed back to Europe, they introduced chocolate fondue to the Swiss nation, where it received a ready welcome.

For chocolate fondue, use the best chocolate available. Chocolate is commonly divided into two groups: pure and compound. Couverture, the highest grade of pure chocolate, is also known as dipping chocolate and is made from cocoa liqueur and cocoa butter. The more cocoa mass it contains, the darker (and more expensive) it becomes. (Semisweet and bittersweet chocolates fall under this category, but unsweetened chocolate is not suited to these recipes.) By contrast, compound chocolate, which includes most chocolate chips, is made of cocoa powder, plus flavorings and stable vegetable fats. Milk chocolate is dark chocolate diluted with milk. White chocolate is not really chocolate at all, although it is made from cocoa butter, plus milk, sugar, vanilla and lecithin.

Classic chocolate fondue

Serves 6

1/2 cup (4 fl oz/125 ml) cream
2 tablespoons kirsch, triple sec, or brandy
9 oz (280 g) milk chocolate, preferably Swiss, chopped
fruits including: dried pineapple, mango and apple; fresh strawberries and pears; fresh mandarin slices
ladyfingers and profiteroles

In a double boiler over simmering water, heat the cream and liqueur or brandy. Add chocolate all at once, stirring until smooth. Transfer to a warmed stoneware or metal fondue pot and accompany with the fruits and sweets. Spear a piece of fruit with a fondue fork and dip the ladyfingers or profiteroles into the pot by hand.

White Chocolate and Coconut Fondue

Serves 6

½ cup (4 fl oz/125 ml) sweetened
  condensed milk

2 tablespoons triple sec

½ cup (4 fl oz/125 ml) thick coconut
  cream

8 oz (250 g) white chocolate, chopped

pinch of ground cinnamon

1 tablespoon flaked dried (desiccated)
  coconut

cookies (biscuits) such as coconut
  macaroons

tropical fruits such as mango, papaya
  (paw paw), pineapple, strawberries,
  lichees, cut into bite-sized chunks

In a double boiler over simmering water, heat milk, liqueur, and coconut cream.
Add chocolate all at once, stirring until melted. Transfer to a warmed stoneware
or metal fondue pot and sprinkle with the cinnamon and dried coconut. Dip
macaroons by hand and skewer fruit with a fondue fork and immerse in the pot.

Butterscotch Fondue

Serves 6

4 tablespoons (2 oz/60 g) unsalted
    butter
2/3 cup (5 fl oz/160 ml) light corn syrup
2/3 cup (5 fl oz/160 ml) cream

1 1/4 cups (9 oz/280 g) firmly packed
    light brown sugar
1 teaspoon vanilla extract (essence)
fruits and cookies (biscuits) of choice

In a medium saucepan, melt butter over medium heat. Add corn syrup and
brown sugar, stirring until just dissolved. Bring to a boil and cook for 2–3
minutes. Remove from stove, then slowly stir in the cream and vanilla. Transfer
to a warm fondue pot, and serve with fruit and cookies.

Gingered dark chocolate fondue

Serves 6

12 oz (375 g) jar candied ginger in syrup (see note)

1/4 cup evaporated milk

1–2 tablespoons rum

6 oz (180 g) semisweet (plain) chocolate, chopped

fruits including: crystallized ginger pieces, candied (glacéed) and fresh cherries, dried pineapple, mango, and papaya, glazed apricots, cut into thick strips, dates, hulled strawberries, and pear slices

Drain ginger and reserve the liquid. (If it has totally crystallized, place it in a pan of warm water over low heat until melted, or in a microwave for 10 seconds.) Reserve the ginger pieces for later.

In a double boiler over simmering water, combine ginger syrup, milk, rum, and chocolate. Stir until melted. Transfer to a warmed stoneware or metal fondue

pot. Skewer pieces of ginger or fruit on fondue forks and dip in the chocolate sauce. Remove and eat.

NOTE Candied ginger in syrup is available at Asian supermarkets. If unavailable, use crystallized ginger and add 1/2 teaspoon ground (powdered) ginger to chocolate.

Rocky road fondue

Serves 6
9 oz (280 g) milk chocolate, chopped
1/2 cup (4 fl oz/125 ml) sweetened condensed milk
1/2 cup (4 fl oz/125 ml) cream
1 tablespoon strong brewed coffee
1 tablespoon rum (optional)
8 oz (250 g) large marshmallows
1/2 cup (2½ oz/75 g) unsalted mixed nuts, lightly toasted and finely ground
pitted dates, ladyfingers, and cookies (biscuits), for serving

In a double boiler over simmering water, combine chocolate, milk, cream, coffee, and rum (if using). Stir until melted. Transfer to a warm fondue pot. Cut half the marshmallows in half, reserving the remaining whole marshmallows for

the serving platter. At the table, briefly stir the cut marshmallows and all of the nuts into the melted chocolate. Serve the remaining marshmallows on a platter, along with the dates and cookies. Skewer them on fondue forks and dip into the chocolate sauce.

NOTE To toast nuts, preheat oven to 375°F (190°C/Gas 5). Spread nuts on a rimmed baking sheet and bake until lightly browned, 8–12 minutes.

Make Your Own...

Anchovy sauce

Makes about ¾ cup (6 fl oz/180 ml)
2-oz (60-g) can anchovy fillets, drained
¼ cup (2 fl oz/60 ml) milk
4 tablespoons (2 oz/60 g) butter
½ cup (4 fl oz/125 ml) olive oil
2 garlic cloves, very finely chopped
¼ teaspoon coarsely ground pepper
½ cup (¾ oz/20 g) chopped fresh
  parsley
salt to taste

In a small bowl, soak anchovy fillets in milk for about 15 minutes. Drain and discard milk. Finely chop anchovies. In a small saucepan, melt butter with oil over medium heat. Add garlic and sauté until fragrant, about 2 minutes; do not brown. Reduce heat to medium low. Add anchovies and pepper and cook for 15 minutes. Stir in parsley and salt. Serve warm.

Chicken broth

Makes 8–10 cups
1 chicken (about 3 lb/1½ kg),
  preferably stewing (steamer) hen,
  whole or cut up
about 12 cups (96 fl oz/3 L) cold water
½-inch (12-mm) piece fresh ginger,
  thinly sliced
2 scallions (shallots/spring onions)
  white part only, chopped and washed
  well
1 tablespoon soy sauce

Rinse chicken well under cold running water. Put in a narrow, tall stock pot and add water to just cover the chicken. Bring to a boil over medium heat, uncovered. Skim to remove the foam. Add ginger, scallions, and soy sauce. Reduce heat to a simmer and cook for about 1½ hours; strain and let cool. Cover and refrigerate overnight. Remove and discard the congealed fat.

Mounted béarnaise

Makes about 2 cups
(16 fl oz/500 ml)

4 tablespoons (2 fl oz/60 ml) dry white wine

3 eggs, separated

3 tablespoons tarragon vinegar

2 shallots (French shallots), very finely chopped

2 teaspoons chopped fresh tarragon, or 1 teaspoon dried tarragon¹/₂ teaspoon coarsely ground pepper

¹/₂ teaspoon salt

³/₄ cup (6 oz/185 g) Clarified butter (see page 56), melted and cooled to room temperature

1 tablespoon chopped fresh parsley

1 teaspoon chopped fresh chervil (optional)

In a small bowl, beat 2 tablespoons of wine into the egg yolks and set aside. In a large bowl, beat egg whites until stiff, glossy peaks form; set aside.

In a small saucepan, combine remaining 2 tablespoons wine, vinegar, shallots, tarragon, and pepper. Boil until reduced to a glaze, about 5 minutes. Let cool.

Whisk in the egg yolks and salt. Set the saucepan in a skillet of barely simmering water. Whisk constantly until mixture is thick and creamy. Remove from heat and very gradually whisk in the melted butter, returning pan to the simmering water periodically to keep the sauce warm. Gently fold in the beaten egg whites, parsley, and if using, chervil. Serve warm.

Nuoc cham

Makes about 1 cup (8 fl oz/250 ml)

2 small garlic cloves

2 small fresh red chilies, seeded and chopped

1¹/₂ tablespoons sugar

juice of 1 lime

¹/₄ cup (2 fl oz/60 ml) fish sauce

¹/₂ cup (4 fl oz/125 ml) water

In a mortar, mash garlic and chili together with a pestle to make a paste. Add all remaining ingredients and stir until dissolved.

Clarified butter

Makes about 3 cups (28 oz/800 g)
2 lb (1 kg) unsalted butter

In a double boiler over simmering water, melt butter. Remove from heat and let sit so the milk solids settle to the bottom. Skim off any foam. Carefully pour or ladle clear yellow liquid through a sieve lined with cheesecloth (muslin), leaving white solids in pan. Store in a sealed jar, and refrigerate.

Enriched meat stock

1 pig's foot
quantity of Chicken broth (see page 54)
1 lb (500 g) cubed pork shoulder
celery leaves (optional)
1 chopped carrot
1/2 teaspoon peppercorns (optional)
1 bay leaf (optional)
salt to taste

Blanch pig's foot in boiling water for 1 minute; drain. Add to chicken stock in a pot with pork shoulder. For Western dishes, add celery leaves, carrot, peppercorns, and bay leaf, plus salt to taste; leave out for Asian ones.

Mizutaki sauce

Makes 1 cup (8 fl oz/250 ml)
2 eggs
1/4 cup (2 fl oz/60 ml) rice vinegar
1/2 teaspoon dry (powdered) mustard
1/3 cup (3 fl oz/90 ml) good-quality oil
    such as grapeseed or cold-pressed
    vegetable
pinch of salt

In a blender, combine all the ingredients and process until frothy, about 5 seconds. Spoon the sauce into individual dipping bowls.

Mongolian firepot dip

Makes 1 cup (8 fl oz/250 ml)
3/4 cup (6 fl oz/180 ml) soy sauce
1/4 cup (2 fl oz/60 ml) peanut oil
1 tablespoon grated fresh ginger
**1 scallion (shallot/spring onion), finely
  chopped**
**2 tablespoons coarsely chopped fresh
  cilantro (fresh coriander)**
pinch of cayenne pepper (optional)

In a small saucepan, bring soy sauce and oil to a boil over high heat. Immediately remove from heat and add ginger and onion. Let cool and pour into individual sauce dishes. Just before serving, add the cilantro and cayenne, if using.

Curried mayonnaise

Makes about 1 1/2 cups
(12 fl oz/375 ml)
2 eggs at room temperature
1 tablespoon fresh lemon juice
1 teaspoon salt
1/4 teaspoon finely ground white pepper
1 cup (8 fl oz/250 ml) peanut oil
1/2 cup (4 fl oz/125 ml) olive oil
1 tablespoon curry powder
1 teaspoon dijon mustard

In a food processor, combine 1 whole egg and 1 egg yolk (reserve egg white for another use), lemon juice, salt, and pepper. Process for 5 seconds. With the machine running, very gradually drizzle in the oil in a very thin stream to make a thick sauce. Add curry powder and mustard and process until very thick.

Quick ponzu

Makes about 2/3 cup (5 fl oz/150 ml)
1/2 cup (4 fl oz/125 ml) soy sauce
2 1/2 tablespoons fresh lemon juice

In a small bowl, combine all ingredients. Pour into individual dipping bowls. Serve the same day it is made.

Glossary

ALE Traditionally, ale was made without hops, and therefore lacked the slight bitterness of beer. Today, there is little difference between ale and other beers. Substitute lager.

APPENZELLER One of the three most common Swiss cheeses, its aroma is slightly spicy, with hints of fermenting fruit. Although it may have a few large holes, they will not be as prevalent as in Emmentaler.

BEAUFORT Regarded as the finest of the French Gruyère cheese family. See Gruyère and Emmentaler.

BLUE An internal-mold cheese with green–blue-colored veining. The classic blue is French Roquefort, made from sheep's milk. Other blues are commonly made from cow's milk, and more rarely goat. Although varying in taste and texture, blue cheeses are largely interchangeable in most recipes. Other notable blues include Gorgonzola from Italy, which sometimes comes blended with mascarpone; bleu de Bresse; fourme d'Ambert; English stilton; and a plethora of crumbly cow's-milk blues.

CANTAL This cheese could loosely be called the French version of Cheddar, although it has a delicately sour under-taste. Use interchangeably with mild to medium Cheddar.

CELLOPHANE NOODLES Commonly known as bean threads, these very thin strands are generally made from mung beans. Soak in hot to boiling water until translucent before using. Cellophane noodles can easily be discerned from rice noodles by their pliable elasticity. Brittle rice noodles break easily; bean noodles do not.

CHESHIRE A traditional English cow's-milk cheese. Like Cheddar, this was originally a cloth-wrapped cartwheel, but is now more commonly made into a rectangular shape.

CIDER, HARD Fermented apple juice, not to be confused with nonalcoholic apple cider. European apple cider commonly tastes bone dry, with little or no residual sugar or fresh fruit flavor. This is the preferred style to use in fondue.

COCONUT MILK/CREAM Canned (tinned) unsweetened coconut milk and cream is available at all Asian grocers and most supermarkets. Do not use sweetened "cream of coconut," which is specially created for desserts or alcohol drinks. When purchasing coconut milk and cream, note that "cream" is the thickest, "milk" is thinner, and "water" refers to the watery liquid in the center of a coconut shell. When a label fails to clearly identify the product, shake the can. The thicker it is, the less it will splash. Once home, place the can in the refrigerator and the richest portion will rise to the top; carefully spoon it off.

COLBY A washed-curd cow's-milk cheese, colby cheese originated in America. The cheese is soft and slightly elastic, and innocuously mild.

COMTÉ A member of the French Gruyère cheese family, Comté has pea-sized holes. See also Gruyère and Emmentaler.

EDAM Easily identifiable because of its red ball shape, Edam is usually sold young. Its texture is creamy and flavor mild. Aged Edam, although rare, has a good flavor when melted.

EMMENTALER The famous holey cheese of Switzerland, Emmentaler is often confused with the hole-less Gruyère. Although similar, the aroma of Emmentaler is sweeter, and its texture smoother and more elastic.

FETA The best and creamiest feta cheeses are made from sheep's and goat's milk; cow's-milk feta is much firmer. Feta is brined and so is very salty, with a distinct tang.

FISH SAUCE A salty, pungent Southeast Asian seasoning made from fermented fish. It is especially popular in Thailand and Vietnam, where it is known as nam pla and nuoc mam, respectively.

FONTINA A mild and creamy cheese from Italy, fontina becomes soft at room temperature. It has the sweetness of Emmentaler and the tang of Gruyère, and a suggestion of Port-Salut. It can be substituted with a young version of any of those cheeses, a Tilsit, or preferably, a Fribourg vacherin.

GALANGALE A rhizome related (and similar) to fresh ginger, galangale is especially popular in Thai dishes.

GORGONZOLA See Blue.

GOUDA A Dutch cow's-milk cheese resembling a strong-tasting Edam. When young, this is a mild-tasting cheese, creamy in texture, faintly sweet and fruity. Mature Gouda, aged for 18 months, becomes granular and easy to grate.

GRUYÈRE A firm to hard cow's-cheese from Switzerland, nutty yet earthy in character. Confusingly, "Gruyère" is also often used to describe similar French mountain cheeses such as Comté, Beaufort, and Emmental. Unlike Emmentaler and Swiss-style variants, Gruyère has no holes.

MONTEREY JACK A very mild white cheese made from cow's milk. Popular in the United States, this cheese is used in Southwestern Tex-Mex and Cal-Mex dishes. Substitute colby, mozzarella, or Münster.

JARSLBERG See Swiss-style cheese.

KIMCHI A Korean pickle, usually cabbage but also radish, fermented and fiery with chili.

KIRSCH A clear cherry distillate, or eau-de-vie.

KONBU A variety of dried kelp from Japan, and an essential ingredient in the Japanese stock known as dashi.

LANCASHIRE English cow's-cheese, crumbly and mild, but sharper with age. Use as a substitute for Cheddar in Welsh rarebit.

MASCARPONE A cultured-cream, with a sweet yet slightly acidic taste. Traditionally made from the cream skimmed during the manufacture of Parmesan cheese.

PARMESAN A hard, strong-tasting cheese used as a topping and a flavoring.

PIZZA CHEESE Grated cheese sold generically in supermarkets, usually a blend of one or more cheeses, such as mozzarella, colby, mild Cheddar, and sometimes Parmesan. Depending on the blend—especially when there is a dominant Cheddar or Parmesan content—this cheese may prove unreliable in a fondue.

PORTER Traditionally a blend of pale beer, brown beer, and stale ale, porter is similar to stout, but not so strong. If unavailable, use stout.

PORT-SALUT A semi-soft cow's-cheese with a bright orange rind. Slightly nutty, it is milder in taste than it looks. Originally, it was made by monks in France. Substitute a Chaumes or St Paulin.

PROVOLONE Commonly sold in large, white-waxed balls or huge cylinders, tied with a cord and hanging from a rack. This cow's-milk cheese, originally from Italy, is now widely manufactured overseas. Young provolone is mild and supple; aged provolone is strong and pungent.

RACLETTE Versions of this cow's-milk cheese, originally from the Valais, are today made abroad. Their taste is usually less well aged and distinct than that of their Swiss counterparts. Raclette cheese has a creamy consistency that melts easily but does not run. Semi-firm cheeses such as Tilsit and German-style Münster may be substituted. Raclette is also served as a table cheese.

RICE PAPER Thin and brittle sheets made from rice starch. These require soaking before use. Round rice paper are known in Vietnamese as bénh tráng, and are available from Asian grocery stores.

RICE VINEGAR A mild vinegar, especially popular in east Asia. Rice vinegar does not have as strong an acidity as Western vinegar. Do not substitute with seasoned rice vinegar, or with Chinese black vinegar, which is usually made from wheat, millet, and sorghum.

RICE WINE Chinese cooking wine is brewed from glutinous rice and millet. Japanese sake, although more expensive, may be substituted, as may dry sherry. Chinese Shaoxing wine, although made from rice, may prove too dominant in flavor, as it is well aged. Do not substitute sweetened rice wines, such as Japanese mirin.

SAPSAGO (SCHABZIEGER) A hard, green-imbued cone-shaped cheese, assertive in flavor. Freshly grated Parmesan has a similar texture—but not flavor—to Sapsago, and may be substituted.

SOY SAUCE Chinese light soy sauce is similar to standard Japanese soy sauce. Do not use Chinese dark or thick soy sauce. All Japanese soy sauces in the international market are naturally brewed, not chemically manufactured.

STOUT A very dark to black beer, renowned for its creamy head. Its faintly sweet taste is countered with the bitterness of hops. The most famous brand of stout is Guinness.

SWISS-STYLE CHEESE A generic cheese only faintly resembling Emmentaler, with large holes. Generally it has little pronounced flavor, and it is available in small rectangles. A good substitute is Norwegian Jarslberg.

TILSIT A firm cow's-milk cheese of both Dutch and German heritage. It is faintly piquant and similar in taste to Gouda, although the primary difference is its washed rind that forms into a hard crust.

TOMME, OR TOME A generic term for cheese, commonly (but not exclusively) the hard mountain styles such as Beaufort. The celebrated tomme de Savoie is made from cow's milk, while a distant Pyrenees version may be sheep's milk. Both cheeses can be used in fondues.

VACHERIN Fribourg vacherin, or vacherin fribourgeois, is a creamier version of Gruyère, yet its flavor is less savory. Substitute French reblochon. The similarly named "vacherin Mont d'Or" is not interchangeable.

Index

....

Cover picture: Crab and cheddar fondue, see page 20
Pictured on page 2: Greek lamb fondue, see page 33
Pictured on page 4: Classic Neuchatel fondue, see page 16

A LANSDOWNE BOOK

Published by Apple Press
Sheridan House
4th Floor
112-116 Western Road
Hove
East Sussex BN3 1DD UK

Created and produced by Lansdowne Publishing
Text: Robert Carmack
Photographer: Louise Lister
Stylist: Kristen Anderson
Designer: Avril Makula
Editor: Joanne Holliman
Production Manager: Sally Stokes
Project Coordinator: Kate Merrifield

ISBN 1 84092 428 4

Set in Trade Gothic, Journal Text, Gill Sans and Neuropol on QuarkXPress
Printed in Singapore by Kyodo Printing Pte Ltd